The Body Language of Love

Allan and Barbara Pease books Published by
Manjul Publishing House in India

- *Body Language in the Work Place*
- *The Definitive Book of Body Language*
- *Why Men Can Do Only One Thing at a Time and Women Never Stop Talking*
- *Why Men Don't Listen and Women Can't Read Maps*
- *Why Men Lie and Women Cry*
- *Why Men Want Sex and Women Need Love*
- *How Compatible Are You?*
- *You Can! People Skills for Life*
- *Questions are the Answers*

The Body Language of Love

Allan + Barbara Pease

Manjul Publishing House

First published in India by

Manjul Publishing House Pvt. Ltd.
Corporate Office:
2nd Floor, Usha Preet Complex,
42 Malviya Nagar, Bhopal, INDIA-462 003
E-mail: manjul@manjulindia.com
Website: www.manjulindia.com
Marketing Office:
7/32, Ground Floor, Ansari Road, Daryaganj, New Delhi 110 002
Email: booksupplyco@gmail.com

The Body Language of Love by *Allan* and *Barbara Pease*

This edition first published in 2012

Copyright © 2012 by Allan Pease
All rights reserved.
Published by agreement with Pease International Pty. Ltd. Australia,
c/o Dorie Simmonds Agency Ltd.

ISBN   978-81-8322-283-9

This edition is authorised for sale in the following countries:
India, Pakistan, Bangladesh, Nepal, Bhutan, Myanmar & Sri Lanka

Printed & bound in India by Thomson Press (India) Ltd.

All rights reserved. No part of this publication may be
reproduced, stored in or introduced into a retrieval system, or transmitted, in any
form, or by any means (electronic, mechanical, photocopying, recording or
otherwise) without the prior written permission of the publisher. Any person
who does any unauthorized act in relation to this publication may be liable to
criminal prosecution and civil claims for damages.

This book is dedicated to all people who have good eyesight but who cannot see.

Acknowledgements

Thank you to those who contributed to this book, whether they knew it or not: Kelly Bradtke, Andrew and Joanne Parish, Decima McAuley, Rebecca Schell, Melissa Stewart, Jasmine Pease, Cameron Pease, Brandon Pease, Bella Pease, Michael Pease, Adam Sellars, John MacIntosh, Norman Leonard, Ken Wright, Amanda Gore, Daniel Clarke, Dr Janet Hall, Col and Jill Haste, Kirsty and Scott Gooderham, Phil Gray, Shirley Neale and Danny Redman, Des Wilmore, Bernie de Souza, Dr James Moir, Helen and Ian Belcher, Roger Loughnan, Ivanna Fugalot, Dr Gennady Polonsky, Christine Walding, Jeff Turner, John Lanesmith, Sally Berghofer, Rob and Sue Keam, Dave Stewart, David C. Smith, Dr John Tickel, Professor Graeme Jackson, Nicole Kilpatrick, Josephine and Rick, Glen Fraser, Tony Rich, Dr Michael Walsh, Angus Woodhead, Fiona Hedger, Gary Crick, Anthony Gorman, Brian Tracy, Jenny Cooper, Ivor Ashfield, Trevor Velt, Jo Abbott, Alan Holliday, Graeme Shiels, Shorty Tully, Kerri-Anne Kennerley, Sue Williams, Janine Good, Bert Newton, Graham Smith, Kevin Fraser, Dr Phillip Stricker, Emma and Graham Steele and Glenda Leonard.

And special thanks to Dorie Simmonds and Ray and Ruth Pease.

Contents

Introduction	1
Understanding the Mating Game: Why Women Hold the Rulebook... and Men Haven't Even Read It	5
How to Play the Mating Game: The Art of Courtship and Flirting Signals	19
How to Make Yourself More Attractive to the Opposite Sex: Using Body Language to Increase Your Mating Rating	49
Speed-Dating, First Dates, Parties, Internet Dating and Other Suicide Missions	75
For Better or for Worse: Finding a Long-Term Mate, Proposing and Dealing with Relationship Problems	103
The Secrets of Successful Relationships	125
Conclusion	151

Some things haven't changed in a million years

Introduction

Everyone knows someone who can walk into a room full of people and, within minutes, have worked out who is single and engaged someone in conversation. They seldom get turned down by the opposite sex, never embarrass themselves (or others) with cheesy chat-up lines, have no problem finding a date and never sit by the phone waiting for it to ring. They just seem to have a gift for understanding the opposite sex and, most importantly, they are skilled at developing enduring relationships. So what's their secret? Put simply, they understand body language and its importance in their love life. Wouldn't you love to be like that? Well, with our help, you will.

At the age of eleven I began my sales career selling rubber sponges door-to-door after school to make pocket money and quickly worked out how to read body language and use it to tell if someone was likely to buy from me or not. I became a successful businessman, but my skills also proved a bonanza for meeting girls in discos. I could nearly always predict who would say yes to a dance with me and who wouldn't. Over the years understanding body language has proved invaluable to my love life and has helped me build an enduring, loving relationship, and it can do the same for you. Unless you have an innate ability or have learned to read body language, however, the chances are you're missing most of it. The skills you'll learn in this book can be used for any aspect of your love life, be it making yourself more attractive to the opposite sex, working out who is attracted to you, going on a date or building a long-term relationship.

ALLAN PEASE

Body language is a fundamental part of courtship because it reveals how available, attractive, ready, enthusiastic, sexy or desperate we are. While some courtship signals are studied and deliberate, others are completely unconscious. It is still unclear how we learn these signals, but research now shows that many may be inborn. It is also a fundamental part of building and preserving a relationship, because it allows us to develop the rapport and sensitivity we need to make one another happy. Anyone can teach themselves to read the signals. That's what *The Body Language of Love* is about.

Most animal species seem to have few problems when it comes to choosing mates and dealing with relationships. For many other species, the female goes on heat, he mates with her, and it's all over. When it comes to choosing a mate for ourselves, however, few humans have much success, let alone any real understanding of the process by which it happens.

Humans are the only species that are confused about the mating game.

Today we are confronted with romantic circumstances that our ancestors never encountered. We can meet new partners through Internet dating agencies, go speed-dating, improve our appearance with cosmetics or surgery, and marry and remarry multiple times. Despite all the choices now open to us, and all the places where we can find love, the world is in the grip of a singles epidemic. By the year 2020 it is estimated that 25% of all women in the Western world will be permanently single. Divorce rates in most places are now around 50%. It's clear that courtship and love remain the least understood aspects of human behaviour, and our failure to understand and read each other's body language is at the heart of the problem.

The Body Language of Love will give you answers to some of the most puzzling questions you've ever had about the opposite sex, and it will change for ever your own behaviour. It will seem as if you've always been in a dark room and, while you could feel the furnishings, the wall hangings and the door, you've never actually seen what they look like. This book will be like turning on the lights to see what was always there. But now you'll know exactly what things are, where they are and what to do about them, and you and your love life will be grateful for it!

BARBARA PEASE

Understanding the Mating Game: Why Women Hold the Rulebook . . . and Men Haven't Even Read It

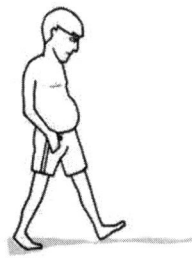 

1. A man and woman approaching on a beach

  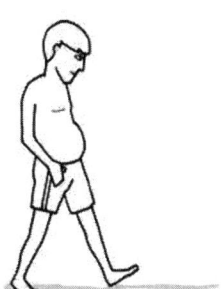

2. They see each other

3. They pass

Your body is already playing the mating game

When we meet people for the first time, we quickly make judgments about their friendliness, dominance and potential as a sexual partner. In fact we form up to 90% of our opinion of their availability and suitability in under 4 minutes. And their eyes are not the first place we look. Body language expert Dr Albert Scheflen found that when a person enters the company of the opposite sex, certain unconscious physiological changes take place. High muscle tone becomes evident in preparation for a possible sexual encounter; the stomach pulls in; the body assumes an erect posture and becomes more youthful-looking. A man will protrude his jaw and expand his chest to make himself appear dominant. A woman who is interested will emphasise her breasts, tilt her head, touch her hair, expose her wrists and thereby make herself appear submissive.

The ideal place to observe this is on a beach when a man and a woman approach each other. The changes take place when they are close enough to make eye contact and will continue until after they have passed. Whether you realise it or not, your body is subconsciously conveying your suitability as a sexual partner. It knows exactly how to play the mating game. So if you want to appeal to the opposite sex, you need to **let your body do the talking**.

> Your body subconsciously responds to the opposite sex to make you more attractive.

Birds do it, bees do it . . . even *you* do it

Male and female animals use a series of intricate courtship gestures, and most of this is done subconsciously. For example, in several species of bird, the male struts around the female giving a vocal display, puffing up his feathers and performing various body movements to gain her attention, while the female appears to display little or no interest. We humans may like to believe we are the most sophisticated species, but our courtship ritual is actually very similar to that performed across nature. In fact, human flirtation involves sequences of gestures and expressions not unlike the courtship dances of animals on wildlife programmes.

The bottom line is that when a person wants to attract the opposite sex, they do so by **emphasising sexual differences**. To discourage the opposite sex, we play down or hide these differences.

> Highlighting gender differences is what makes a person look 'sexy'.

Now, watch a master at work

Graham was a man who had developed a skill that most men would kill to have. He would attend a social function and somehow quickly 'scope out' the available women, make his choice and, in almost record-breaking time, would be seen heading towards the exit with her, escorting her to his car and driving back to his apartment. He seemed to have a built-in radar for finding the available women and getting them to go with him. No one knew how he did it ... except us ...

Graham's technique was first to spot women whose body language indicated they were available and then to respond with his own male courtship gestures. Those who were interested would return the appropriate female signals, giving him the non-verbal green light to proceed to the next stage. Women would describe him as 'sexy', 'humorous' and 'someone who makes me feel feminine'. This was their reaction to the constant attention he'd give them and the courtship signals he used. Men, however, described him as sleazy, arrogant and pushy because of the competition he presented.

> To succeed in the mating game, you must become adept at body language signals.

Why women call the shots . . . and hold the rulebook

Ask any man who usually makes the first move in courtship and he will invariably say that men do. All studies into flirtatious encounters, however, show that women are the initiators 90% of the time. A woman does this by sending a series of subtle eye, body and facial signals to the targeted man, who, assuming he is perceptive enough to pick them up, responds. There are men who will approach women in a club or bar without being sent the green light, but their overall statistical success rate is low because they weren't invited first – they're simply playing the numbers game. To be successful in courtship by playing the numbers game, a man has to approach a lot of women to make a sale – unless, of course, he looks like Brad Pitt.

In courtship, women call the tunes most of the time – men do most of the dancing.

Body Language of Love
Rule No. 1

Any man who crosses the floor to chat up a woman has usually done so at her request after picking up her body language signals. It just looks as if he made the first move because he walked across the floor.

Her Body Language of Love

The success women have in intimate encounters is directly related to their ability to **send courtship signals to men and to decode those being sent back**. Women's difficulty in finding partners is not about reading signals; it's more about finding a man who'll match their criteria.

His Body Language of Love

For a man, success in the mating game relies mainly on his ability to **read the signals being sent to him**, as opposed to being able to initiate his own moves. Most women are aware of courtship signals, but men are far less perceptive, often being completely blind to them, which is why so many men have difficulty finding potential mates.

Why men crash and burn when they approach women...

Most men find it difficult to interpret the more subtle cues in women's body language and research shows that men tend to mistake friendliness and smiling for sexual interest. This is because men see the world in more sexual terms than women; men have 10 to 20 times more testosterone than women, which makes them view everything around them in terms of sex. Men may misinterpret a woman's early signals of interest and make a clumsy sexual pass in a bar or nightclub, which is of course rebuffed and he has to make the walk of shame back across the dance floor to his friends.

To some men, when a lady says 'no', she means maybe; when she says 'maybe', she means 'yes'; but if she says 'yes', she's no lady.

...and why some women never get approached at all

When they meet a possible partner, women send out subtle, but often deceptive, courting signals to see whether he's worth pursuing. Women tend to bombard men with courting rituals in the first minutes of meeting them. By sending erratic and ambiguous signals in the early stages, women manipulate men into showing their hand. This is one reason why many women have trouble attracting men – men become confused and won't make an approach to a woman they are interested in for fear of being rejected.

> A man won't approach a woman unless she gives clear, consistent signals and he can be fairly certain his advance won't be rejected. This explains why many beautiful single women complain that men never chat them up.

> To be an expert in courtship,
> a woman needs to learn how to send out
> the right body language signals,
> while men have to become skilled at
> reading them.

How to Play the Mating Game: The Art of Courtship and Flirting Signals

The attraction process

Human courtship follows a predictable five-step sequence that we all go through when we meet an attractive person.

1. Eye contact: She looks across the room and spots a man she fancies. She waits till he notices her, then holds his gaze for about five seconds and then looks away. He keeps watching her to see if she does it again. A woman needs to deliver this gaze, on average, three times before the average man realises what's happening. This is the start of the flirting process.

2. Smiling: She delivers one or more fleeting smiles. This is a quick half-smile that is intended to give a prospective man the green light to make an approach. Unfortunately, many men are not responsive to these signals, leaving the woman feeling that he's not interested.

3. Preening: She plays with her hair for up to six seconds, suggesting she is grooming herself for her man. She may lick her lips, flick her hair and straighten her clothing and jewellery. He'll respond with gestures such as standing up straight, pulling his stomach in, expanding his chest, adjusting his clothing, touching his hair and tucking his thumbs into his belt or trousers. They both point their feet or entire bodies towards each other.

4. Talk: He approaches and attempts to make small talk, using clichés and ice-breakers such as 'Haven't I seen you somewhere before?'

5. Touch: She looks for an opportunity to initiate a light touch on his arm, either 'accidental' or otherwise. A hand touch indicates a higher level of intimacy than a touch on the arm. Each level of touch is then repeated to check that the man is happy with this level of intimacy and to let him know that the first touch was not accidental. Lightly brushing or touching the shoulder of a man is done to give the impression that the woman cares about his appearance or condition. Shaking hands is a quick way to move to the touch stage.

These first five stages of courtship may seem minor or even incidental but they are critical to starting any new relationship and, as we have seen, are what most men find difficult. If women want to be approached by men, they need to **give clear, unambiguous messages**, and men simply need to **read them and respond.**

The top five *green lights* every man should recognise

Because a man's success in the mating game is largely dependent on how well he can recognise and respond to a woman's signals, it really pays for him to learn how to decode the most commonly used female courtship gestures. In general, when a woman is interested in a man, she will use some **basic preening gestures**, including touching her hair or smoothing her clothing. She might place one or both hands on her hips, point her foot or body towards the man and increase eye contact. Here is a summary of the most common courtship gestures and signals used by women everywhere to show a man that she could be available. Single men who have difficulty in scoping out available women, start taking notes now ...

1. The Head Toss and Hair Flick

This is usually the first display a woman will use when she's around a man she fancies. The head is flicked back to toss the hair over the shoulders or away from the face. Even women with short hair will use this gesture. It's a way for a woman subtly to show that she cares about how she looks to a man. This also lets her expose her armpit, which allows the 'sex perfume' known as pheromone to waft across to the target man.

> Preening the hair lets pheromones in the armpit work their magic.

2. Fondling a Cylindrical Object

Fondling an object, such as her finger, the stem of a wine glass, a dangling earring, a cigarette or any phallic-shaped object, is an unconscious indication of what may be on the mind. Taking a ring off and on the finger can also be a mental representation of having sex. When a woman does these things, a man might respond by symbolically trying to possess her by fondling her cigarette lighter, car keys or any personal item she has nearby. If a woman is doing any of these gestures and looking directly and repeatedly at you, it is your cue to approach.

The stem of the wine glass suggesting things that may yet come

3. Self-Touching

Our minds get our bodies to act out our secret desires – and so it is with **Self-Touching**. Women have significantly more nerve sensors for experiencing touch than men do, making women more sensitive to touch sensations. When a woman slowly and sensually strokes her thigh, neck or throat, it implies that if a man plays his cards right, he may be able to touch her in these same ways. At the same time her self-touch lets her imagine what it might feel like if the man was initiating the touch. This may be accompanied by slowly crossing and uncrossing her legs.

4. The Knee Point and the Shoe Fondle

One leg is tucked under the other and points to the person she finds the most interesting. This is a relaxed position, which takes the formality out of a conversation and gives the opportunity for a fleeting exposure of the thighs.

Pointing her knee at the most interesting person

Dangling the shoe on the end of the foot also indicates a relaxed attitude and has the phallic effect of thrusting the foot in and out of the shoe. This action unsettles many men without them knowing what is happening.

The shoe gives a clue

5. The Face Platter

This courtship gesture is used by a woman who wants to attract a man's attention. She will place one hand on top of the other and present her face to him as if it was on a platter for him to admire.

The Face Platter: presenting her face for a man to admire

Tip: If you are a man and are going to use flattery – sincere or not – this gesture gives the green light for it.

Other come-ons men need to memorise

1. **Handbag in Close Proximity:** A woman's handbag is a personal item that's treated by her almost as if it's an extension of her body and so it becomes a strong signal that she's interested when she puts it close to a man. If she finds him particularly attractive, she may slowly fondle and caress her handbag.

2. **The Limp Wrist:** Walking or sitting while holding a **Limp Wrist** is a submission signal and a great attention-getter. It's very attractive to men because it makes them feel as if they can dominate.

3. **Exposed Wrists:** An interested woman will gradually expose the smooth, soft underside skin of her wrists to the potential male partner and will increase the rate she flashes her wrists as her interest grows. The wrist area has long been considered one of the highly erotic areas of the female body because it is one of the more delicate skin areas.

4. Sideways Glance Over Raised Shoulder: The **Raised Shoulder** is self-mimicry of the rounded female breasts. With partially drooped eyelids, the woman holds the man's gaze just long enough for him to notice, then quickly looks away. This action produces the feeling of peeping in the woman who does it and being peeped at by the man who receives it.

How to grab a man's attention

When people approach each other from a distance, they look quickly between the other person's face and lower body to establish what the sex of the person is and then a second time to determine the level of interest in them. This is called an **Intimate Gaze**. Men and women use this gaze to show interest in each other, and those who are interested will return the gaze.

When men use the Intimate Gaze, it's usually blatantly obvious to women, but because women have wider peripheral vision, men are generally unaware of having been given an Intimate Gaze, much to the frustration of the woman who gave it.

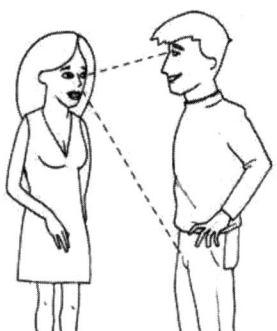

Women's wider peripheral vision means never getting caught; men's tunnel vision means always getting caught

**Tip:** Most men are not hardwired to read a woman's first gaze signal, so she usually needs to repeat it three times before the average man picks up on it, four times for really slow men and five or more times for the especially thick. When she finally gets his attention, she can use a small version of the **Eyebrow Flash** – a subtle eye-widening gesture that tells him the signal was intended for him. Sometimes a face-to-face verbal approach of 'Hey, I like you!' is more effective on men who are slow on the uptake.

> Despite most people's strong denials, hidden camera studies reveal that everyone practises the Intimate Gaze, including nuns.

And the top three *red lights* every man should recognise

Bob gazed across the room and locked eyes with an attractive brunette. She seemed to smile at him and, not being slow on the uptake, he swiftly crossed the room and began a conversation with her. She didn't seem to talk much but she was still smiling at him, so he persisted. One of his female friends sauntered past and whispered, 'Forget it, Bob . . . she thinks you're a jerk.' He was stunned. But she was still smiling at him! As with most men, Bob didn't understand the negative significance of the tight-lipped, no-teeth-visible female smile.

Because so many men cite fear of a humiliating rejection as the reason they so infrequently approach women, it pays for men to learn to spot the main no-go gestures used by women to tell men they are not interested.

1. The Tight-Lipped Smile

The lips are stretched tight across the face to form a straight line and the teeth are concealed. It sends the message that the smiler has a secret or a withheld opinion or attitude that they will not be sharing with you. It's a favourite of women who don't want to reveal that they don't like the man they are talking to and is usually clearly read by other women as a rejection signal. Most men are oblivious to it.

2. Crossed Arms

Hiding behind a barrier is a normal response we learn at an early age to protect ourselves. As children, we hid behind solid objects such as furniture or our mother's skirt whenever we found ourselves in a threatening situation. As we grew older, this hiding behaviour became more sophisticated. As adults, we fold one or both arms across the chest in an unconscious attempt to block out what we perceive as a threat or undesirable circumstances. Women's use of arm barriers is less noticeable than men's because women can grasp on to things like handbags or purses.

The handbag is used to tell a man that she isn't interested – he should move on and retain his dignity

> **Women tend to keep their arms open when they are around men they find attractive and are likely to fold their arms across their breasts around aggressive or unattractive men.**

3. Leaning Away

Moving close to, or into the **Intimate Zone** of, the opposite sex is a way of showing interest in that person and is commonly called an 'advance'. If the advance into the Intimate Zone is rejected, the other person will step back to reclaim their space.

A space-invading man forcing a woman to lean back to defend her space

The above illustration shows the negative reaction of a woman on whose territory a man is encroaching. She leans backward, attempting to keep a comfortable distance. This is a man's cue to walk away or try a different tack.

Her Body Language of Love

Women who wear short skirts will sit with their legs tightly crossed for protection, but this results in them looking less approachable and are less likely to be asked to dance at a nightclub. Men love to see a woman's legs, but choose clothes that you are comfortable in and that do not restrict your body language.

> **Mini-skirts can give a woman the appearance that she's not approachable.**

His Body Language of Love

Research has shown that women fear attack from behind and are wary of approaches from the rear. If you are male, therefore, it's better to approach a woman you are interested in from the front and eventually you can angle yourself to 45 degrees, which helps to create rapport and is less confrontational than facing her head on.

The top three *green lights* every woman should recognise

If you're a woman, you'll probably be disappointed with our summary of male courtship signals because there aren't too many. As with most male animals, the human male displays **preening behaviour** as a potential partner arrives on the scene. He will straighten his tie, smooth his collar, brush imaginary dust from his shoulder, touch his cufflinks or watch, and rearrange his shirt and other clothing. When it comes to courtship rituals, though, most men are as effective as someone standing in a river trying to catch fish by hitting them on the head with a big stick. Women have more lures and fishing skills to land their fish than any male could ever hope to acquire.

Male displays involve the show of power, wealth and status. Men rev their car engines, brag about how much they earn and challenge other men.

Men are generally not good at sending the signals used in the mating game and, as we mentioned earlier, women not only control the game, they hold the rulebook. Men simply react to signals they see. Being ahead of the game at reading body language, most women don't need help in identifying when a man is interested, but here are some dead giveaways.

1. Protruding Thumbs

Thumbs denote superiority. In palmistry, the thumbs represent strength of character and the ego, and body language signals involving the thumbs also show self-important, confident attitudes. Thumbs are used to display dominance and assertiveness. A man will use **Protruding Thumbs** around women to whom he is attracted. Thumb-Displayers also often rock on the balls of their feet to give the impression of extra height. Thumbs sometimes protrude from the back pockets as if the person is trying to hide their dominant attitude.

Thumb-Displayers often try to conceal their confident, authoritative attitude, but he's clearly interested

2. Crotch Display

The Crotch-Displayer plants both feet firmly on the ground, making a clear statement that he has no intention of leaving. It highlights the genitals, giving the Crotch-Displayer a macho-looking attitude.

> The Crotch Display is used by macho men and tough guys.

He may also turn his body towards her, point his foot at her and hold her gaze for longer than usual. When he's seated or leaning against a wall, he may spread his legs to display his crotch. Monkeys and chimps do it too.

The crotch diplay – putting his masculinity on show

3. The Cowboy Stance

Thumbs tucked into the belt or into the tops of the pockets frames the genital area and is a display used mainly by men to show a sexually aggressive attitude. Also jokingly called the **Man-of-the-Long-Thumbs** gesture, the arms take the readiness position and the hands serve as central indicators, highlighting the crotch. Men use this gesture to stake their territory or to show other men that they are unafraid. Apes use the same gesture, but without a belt or trousers.

This gesture tells others, 'I am virile – I can dominate,' which is why it's a regular for men on the prowl. Any man talking to a woman while he's standing like this – with his pupils dilated and one foot pointing towards her – is easily read by most women. It's one of the gestures that gives the game away for men, as they unwittingly declare what's on their mind.

The Cowboy Stance – his fingers point at what he wants you to notice

He's coming on strong – foot forward, legs apart, Crotch Display and Arms-Splayed to try to enlarge his overall perceived size and take up more space – but she's using typical female no-go body language: legs together, body facing away, arms folded and minimising the amount of space she occupies. He's going home alone

Body Language of Love
Rule No. 2

Women become more sexually active in the middle of their menstrual cycle when they are ovulating and are most likely to conceive. It's during this time that they are more likely to wear shorter dresses and higher heels to walk, talk, dance and act more provocatively, and to display the signals discussed in this chapter.

Her Body Language of Love

To measure a man's level of interest in her, a woman will step into his Intimate Zone and then step back out again. If he's interested, this cues him to step into her space whenever he makes a point. Once again, the woman is the one who calls the shots in the flirting stakes.

His Body Language of Love

Women everywhere complain that they will be talking with a man and suddenly, for no apparent reason, he will begin adjusting or handling his crotch. The inference is that his genitals are so large and cumbersome that they need constant attention to prevent the cut-off of blood circulation. Most women can't imagine being in a public place and reaching down to scratch their crotch and are amazed that men will do this nonchalantly and with regularity. Women are horrified when a man proceeds to get her a drink using the same hand he just used for his adjustments and then greets people with a handshake. Men should avoid the Crotch Adjust when in a woman's company.

> **The Crotch Adjust is one of women's number one turn-offs.**

How to Make Yourself More Attractive to the Opposite Sex:
Using Body Language to Increase Your Mating Rating

Bob was popular. He was the only man in the nudist camp who could carry four coffees and ten doughnuts

Enhance and improve appearance

Like it or not, the way we look affects our ability to attract, and keep, a partner. People we meet form up to 90% of their opinion about us within the first 4 minutes, and our physical desirability is assessed in less than 10 seconds. This is not to say that because you don't look like Heidi Klum or Brad Pitt you can't do well with the opposite sex. But by understanding how the process of attraction works, and then employing some simple strategies to use it to your advantage, you can easily become more alluring.

Ancient biological gender signals operate on a subconscious level, and we just can't help responding to them. Fundamentally, both men's and women's brains are wired to be attracted to those who show the most **healthy reproductive ability and sexual availability**. The good news is that you don't need to be naturally or stereotypically good-looking to attract the opposite sex. Studies have found that we prefer to find mates who are roughly as attractive as we are, rather than better-looking than us because more attractive partners

> Highlighting your sexual differences and your availability will make you more attractive to the opposite sex.

are more likely to stray or look for a better offer. To attract the opposite sex, a woman mainly needs to be able to display the signs that she is healthy and could be available, while a man needs to highlight his vitality and virility. This is why some men and women who are not particularly physically attractive seem to have plenty of suitors.

Why women shouldn't despair

Some women are appalled at the idea of 21st-century men being initially attracted to a woman based on her appearance and availability instead of wanting her for her ability to nurture, communicate, be a domestic goddess or play the piano. But the reality is that you need to attract a man first before he can find out about all your inner virtues. When you go fishing, you bait the hook with what the fish likes, not with what you like. Have you ever tasted a worm? You might be repulsed by the thought, but for a fish, it's his favourite dish.

Women spend 3 times as much time as men on their physical appearance and 15 times as much on products to maintain that appearance. Women who fail to do this lose their edge in the mating game. A myriad of deceptive visual aids are used by women to attract men. These include wearing artificial fingernails to make the hands look longer, breast implants to look more youthful, dark clothing or vertical stripes to appear thinner, dyeing their hair blonde, wearing high heels and padding their clothing. The reason these strategies work is because they appeal to the mating preferences hardwired into male brains. It's not that *women* necessarily want to do these things; it's because *men* want them to and women know it. Remember, you don't need to look like Angelina Jolie, or model yourself on her, but by highlighting your sexual difference and looking more available, you will be more attractive to men. None of this is Politically Correct – but it is all Biologically Correct.

Why women should... tilt their pelvis

Medical evidence shows that a woman in excellent health and most capable of successfully bearing children has a **hips-to-waist ratio** of 70%; that is, her waist is 70% the size of her hips. This gives her what's known as an hourglass figure. Throughout recorded history this is the body ratio that has proved the most dramatic male attention-grabber. The way a woman highlights this ratio is simple – she tilts her pelvis when she stands.

> Tilting the pelvis while standing highlights a woman's ability to bear children successfully.

One experiment found that men gave women with the 70% hips-to-waist ratio the highest rating even when the woman's weight was quite heavy. This means a woman can be physically larger but will still turn male heads if she has this ratio.

Why women should . . . wear eye make-up and contact lenses

In almost every country large eyes are considered attractive. Make-up achieves the effect of enlarging the eye and recreating an infantile look. If eyes look larger relative to the lower face, they will engender protective feelings in men. When a woman finds a man attractive, her pupils dilate, and mascara, eye shadow and eyeliner all artificially create a permanent state of looking interested. Men are more attracted, however, to a woman who wears natural-looking make-up than one who looks as if she applied it with a bricklayer's trowel.

Contact lenses give the illusion a woman's eyes are glistening and have dilated pupils, which explains why photographic experiments show a man finds a woman 'strangely attractive' when she wears contact lenses.

The female cosmetics and toiletry industry has become worth, globally, more than $50 trillion a year – and all with the purpose of creating the illusion of facial sexual signals.

Why women should . . . wear heels

> High heels lengthen a woman's legs, make her buttocks sway and her breasts jut out.

Men love high heels on a woman because they enhance a woman's sexual shape by lengthening her legs, arching her back, forcing her buttocks to protrude, making her feet appear smaller and thrusting her pelvis forward. This is why the shoe with the highest heel – the stiletto – with its bondage straps, is by far the most efficient sex aid on the market. Men like women's legs to look athletic and shapely, as fat in the legs is an indicator of better lactation, but he will be turned off if she looks like she could play football for England.

Also, when a woman walks, she has a marked roll to her gait, which highlights her pelvic region. Wearing heels accentuates this wiggle and wearing tight designer jeans draws attention to her protruding buttocks.

Marilyn Monroe reputedly chopped three-quarters of an inch off the heel of her left shoe to emphasise her wiggle.

Why women should... subtly emphasise their cleavage

Most of the breast consists of fat tissue. This gives them their rounded shape, and most of this tissue is not involved in milk production. Overall, breasts serve one clear purpose – sexual signalling. Breasts mimic a woman's rear view – a relic from the days when humans walked on all fours.

Low-cut dresses and push-up bras emphasise this signal by creating cleavage. Fortunately, nearly all sex research surveys show that men love breasts in most shapes and sizes. It's the cleavage that stimulates men the most; it doesn't matter whether a woman's breasts are the size of small lemons or look like watermelons. A woman who is attracted to a man is likely to lean forward and bring her arms closer to her body, which presses her breasts together and makes a cleavage. Don't look too obvious, though, or you'll risk looking trashy.

What does an older woman have between her knees that a younger woman doesn't?
Her boobs.

Why women should . . . wear bright red lipstick

For one of our television shows, we asked nine women to turn up for a series of interviews with both male and female interviewers. For half the interviews, each woman wore lipstick, but they did not wear it to the other half. A survey of the interviewers' attitudes after the experiment quickly became clear – the women wearing red lipstick and using larger lip displays were seen as more interested in themselves and in men's attention. This means that a woman should wear larger displays of bright red lipsticks for attracting the opposite sex and going on dates – but never to a job interview.

When a woman becomes sexually aroused, her lips, breasts and genitals become larger and redder as they fill with blood. The use of lipstick is an Egyptian invention that is four thousand years old and is intended to mimic facially the reddened genitals of the sexually aroused female. This explains why men consistently find bright red lipstick the most attractive and sensual. Pouting and licking the lips simply increase the lip display.

Body Language of Love
Rule No. 3

Surveys show that women continually express a preference for men with deeper, smoother voices because deep tones are directly linked to testosterone levels. The change in voice tone is noticeable in boys because when they reach puberty, their bodies flood with male hormones and their voices 'crack' virtually overnight. When a man is around a woman he fancies, he's likely to start speaking in deeper tones to highlight his masculinity, while a responsive woman is likely to start talking in higher-pitched tones to contrast her femaleness.

Body Language of Love
Rule No. 4

When you smile at another person, they will almost always return the smile, which causes positive feelings in both you and them, because of cause and effect. Understandably, therefore, smiling at others and encouraging them to smile at you is an important part of making yourself attractive. Be sure to smile plenty when interacting with the opposite sex, therefore, and if using Internet dating sites, select a profile picture that shows you smiling and happy. Make sure your teeth are visible – a tight-lipped smile signals contempt or secretive attitude. For women, note that photos of you in sultry poses give men the impression you are more interested in casual sex, not a long-term relationship.

> Science has proved that the more you smile, the more positive reactions others will give you and the more attractive you will seem.

Why men should... highlight shoulders, chest and rear

Overall, women look for broad shoulders, muscular chest and arms, and a tight butt. Even in the 21st century, surveys overwhelmingly show women still want a man who looks as if he can wrestle animals and fight off invaders. The male chest developed to house large lungs, enabling more effective distribution of oxygen and allowing him to breathe more efficiently when running and chasing. In primitive tribes, the bigger his chest, the more respect and power a man commanded. Men can highlight their chest and shoulders, and display their arms by wearing fitted T-shirts and tops.

A tight, muscular rear is necessary to make the strong thrusting motion needed for successful sperm transfer during sex. A man with a fat or flabby derrière has difficulty with this forward movement and has a tendency to throw his entire body weight into the thrust, which is uncomfortable for the woman. Tight jeans will display the rear to best effect. Putting your mobile phone or wallet in your back pocket highlights and lifts a flat posterior.

> Male bodies are purpose-built to chase, catch and wrestle animals, carry heavy things and kill spiders.

Why men should... display dominance

In troops of baboons, and with several other primates, males show their dominance by spreading their legs to offer others a full view of the size of their wedding tackle, and by giving it the occasional adjustment from time to time, they can constantly assert their dominant status. This same display is used by human males to assert their manhood, though it is more subtle than the baboons, mainly because of the hefty prison sentence this baboon display would carry.

Tip: Men can achieve the same effect with tight-fitting trousers, small-size Speedo swimming trunks or dangling the long end of a belt or a bunch of keys in front of their crotch.

Why men should . . . try the three-day beard

Male hormones cause facial-hair growth. The higher a man's testosterone on a given day, the faster it grows. Stress and illness suppress testosterone, which is why a sick or stressed man doesn't need to shave very often. Consequently, the three-day beard serves as a strong visual badge of masculinity and health, and can be a real turn-on to women. Most women would agree, for instance, that Brad Pitt looks far sexier with growth on his chin than he does clean-shaven.

The goatee enhances the perceived size of the chin, and strong protruding chins are a sign of masculinity. Unfortunately, the goatee beard owes its origins to Satan, which can make it difficult for a man to gain acceptance and trust, vital when courting a woman. Our advice is to avoid shaving the day of a party and to steer clear of goatees.

Why men should... wear powerful clothing

In one experiment, women were shown photographs of men wearing high-status clothing, such as three-piece suits, navy blazers, white shirts with designer ties and Rolex watches. The women were asked to rate their level of attraction to the men and how likely they would be to have coffee with each man, go on a date with him, have sex with him or marry him. The women were also shown pictures of the same men dressed in low-status clothing, such as T-shirts and jeans, singlets, baseball caps and a Burger King uniform. Overall, the women said they would consider having coffee, dating, having sex or marrying the men in the high-status clothing but would not consider doing the same with the men dressed in the low-status clothing. These experiments have been replicated in other cultures, producing the same results. The bottom line is that the hunter who displays the best hunting skills, has the most cattle or best beads and bracelets gets the most women.

Why men should . . . give their love life an instant lift

Men should stand straight, walk tall, act assertively and wear dark-coloured clothing to gain perceived height. Dr Bruce Ellis, head of Experimental Psychology at the University of Canterbury in New Zealand, found that taller men have greater reproductive success than shorter men, not only because increased testosterone levels are linked to tallness but also because women choose men who are taller than they are as partners. Taller men are seen as more protective and can pass this advantage on through their genes. Men prefer shorter women because it gives men the apparent height advantage.

> You usually see taller men with shorter women but rarely the reverse.

Why men should . . . learn to dance

Many men are not strong in the brain areas required to feel rhythm and so aren't as good at dancing as women. Go to any aerobics class and watch the male participants (if any turn up) trying to keep time. When a man takes dancing lessons for basic rock 'n' roll and waltz, he will be the hit of the party with all women. Dancing has been described as a vertical act of horizontal desire and that's its history – it's a ritual that evolved to allow close male-female body contact as a lead-up to courtship, just as it does with other animals.

Her Body Language of Love

Most men agree that the **Leg Twine** is the most appealing sitting position a woman can take. It's a gesture that women consciously use to draw attention to their legs. Albert Scheflen states that one leg is pressed firmly against the other to give the appearance of high muscle tone, which is a condition that the body takes when a person is ready for sexual performance and makes the skin look healthy and youthful. This is the position taught to women in deportment and modelling classes. Because of the bone configuration of female legs and hips, most men can't sit like this, so it becomes a powerful signal of femininity. Not surprisingly, over 86% of male participants in our leg-rating surveys voted this the most attractive female sitting position.

The Leg-Twine: men's number one female sitting position

His Body Language of Love

Men should avoid putting their hands in their pockets or women will think they are closed off. Keeping their hands concealed is a favourite ploy of men who don't want to participate in a conversation. The palms were originally like the vocal cords of body language because they did more 'talking' than any other body part and putting them away was like keeping one's mouth shut. Showing your hands conveys openness and willingness to engage with others.

Her Body Language of Love

An experiment using 15 photographs of women showing happy, sad and neutral faces were rated for attractiveness by 257 respondents. The women with the sad expressions were considered the least attractive. Pictures of unsmiling women were decoded as a sign of unhappiness, while pictures of unsmiling men were seen as a sign of dominance. Smiling women also appear more submissive and less threatening, making them more approachable to men. In social situations, therefore, and particularly when courting, it definitely pays dividends for women to smile and laugh when talking to a man. Interestingly, because women smile more in general, they are 26% more likely to return smiles from the opposite sex.

> Men find women who smile attractive and approachable.

His Body Language of Love

In courtship, laughing can be used as a way of determining how successfully a couple is likely to bond. Simply put, the more he can make her laugh, the more attractive she will find him. This is because the ability to make others laugh is perceived as a dominant trait and women prefer dominant males. This explains why having a sense of humour is near the top of women's list of what they look for in a man. When a woman says, 'He's such a funny guy. We spent the whole night laughing together,' she usually means that she spent the night laughing and he spent the night making her laugh. The point for men to understand is that humorous men look more attractive. Fortunately, you can learn to be humorous.

> **Studies show that women laugh at men they're attracted to,
> and men are attracted to women who laugh at their jokes.**

Speed-Dating, First Dates, Parties, Internet Dating and Other Suicide Missions

Mark thought the date was going brilliantly, and sat there with his legs wide apart, stroking his tie and massaging the salt shaker. He hadn't noticed that for the past 20 minutes her legs had been crossed away from him and pointing towards the nearest exit

Speed-dating secrets

> Others form up to 90% of their opinion about you in the first four minutes, and 60–80% of the impact you will make is non-verbal.

When it comes to speed-dating, success is all about making a positive first impression. In the same way that making a good impression on an interviewer is essential in getting a job offer, the first 15 seconds of a speed date will most likely decide whether that person wants to see you again or not. In the end, most of what you talk about is forgotten. What is remembered is the impression you made. Here are our five golden rules for getting it right at speed-dating:

1. The Approach

When it is time to approach someone, walk over without hesitation but with a measured pace similar to a march to demonstrate your confidence and enthusiasm about meeting them.

2. The Greeting

Smile and, if a handshake is offered, keep your palm straight and return the pressure you receive. Introduce yourself and use the other person's name twice in the first 15 seconds. Never talk for more than 30 seconds at a time.

'I hope I haven't talked too much'

3. Your Gestures

Mirror the other person's gestures and expressions when appropriate. If you are a woman, avoid using too many facial expressions or you may be thought of as ditsy. Look animated and interested, and make sure you smile and flash your teeth.

4. Distance

Respect the other person's personal space, but don't lean so far back that you seem aloof. If you move too close, the person may respond by sitting back, leaning away or using repetitive gestures such as drumming the fingers.

5. Your Exit

Use the other person's name again when you say your goodbyes. People always watch you from behind as you leave, so if you're a man, make sure you have shined the back of your shoes. This is an area many men neglect and women are critical of this. When a woman decides to leave, she will begin to adjust the back of her clothing and hair so that she makes a good rear-view impression as she departs.

Like it or not, everyone steals a look at a woman's rear when she walks away, even if they don't like her front view.

Body Language of Love
Rule No. 5

The rules for speed-dating are the same as for any initial face-to-face meeting. Essentially, a man wants to check out a woman's hair, legs, body shape and overall presentation. If she maintains eye contact, as women are often taught to do when meeting someone for the first time, it restricts this process, so he's left trying to steal glances at her without getting caught and so can't focus on the conversation. Video cameras also reveal that women go through the same evaluation process, but women's wider peripheral vision means they rarely get caught.

 **Tip:** When you go speed-dating, shake hands and then give the other person a two-to-three-second frame of uninterrupted time for them to complete the process of checking you out. Turn to hang up your coat or bag on the back of your seat, or move your chair in closer, and then look up, slowly.

Five top tips for speed-dating

1. **Practise using positive gestures:** This will improve your self-confidence and others will perceive you in a more positive way.

2. **Nod slowly** when listening to the opposite sex. This shows you are interested in what they are saying. Also tilt your head slightly.

3. **Pay attention to your posture** so you look confident yet interested. Lean forward when listening.

4. **When you gesture,** keep your fingers closed and your hands below chin level.

5. **Avoid crossing your arms** and keep your body language open and approachable.

Our pointers for a perfect first date

1. **Choose a venue with subdued lighting:** If a woman is attracted to a man, she will dilate her pupils at him and his pupils will dilate in response. Research has shown that when pornographic films are shown to men, their pupils can dilate up to three times their size. This is why romantic encounters are successful in dimly lit places, because everyone's pupils dilate and create the impression that couples are interested in each other.

2. **Avoid venues with loud music** or you risk talking louder and louder as the evening progresses to the point where you are yelling at each other. Instead, choose somewhere with ambient background music, which will get you to tap in time together, creating rapport.

3. **Angle your body at 45 degrees to the other person,** so you come across as friendly and open but not too intense. Then you can move to 0 degrees as things get more intimate.

When a man is excited by a woman, which part of his body can grow to almost three times its size?

Creating the right vibes on a date

When a couple is in the early stages of courtship, it's common to see them use synchronous movements, almost as if dancing. For example, when a woman takes a sip of wine, the man wipes the corner of his mouth, or he begins a sentence and she finishes it. When a person says, 'The vibes are right,' or 'the chemistry is good' they are unknowingly referring to synchronous behaviour. For instance, at a restaurant, one person can be reluctant to eat or drink alone for fear of being out of sync. When it comes to ordering, they may first check with their companion. 'What are you having?' they ask as they try to mirror their meals.

Tip: On a date, try subtly mirroring your companion's seating position, body angle, gestures and speech patterns. Before long they'll start to feel that there's something about you they like and find you 'easy to be with'. This is because they see themselves reflected in you.

> People who feel similar emotions will begin to match each other's body language.
> This is called mirroring and says, 'Look at me. I feel the same way as you!'

> Extended gazing can create intimate feelings.

Blind dates . . . the eyes have it

For a television show we conducted an experiment using a dating agency. A selected number of men were told that their next date was well matched to them and that they should expect to have a successful, fun time. We explained to each man that his date had suffered an injury to one eye as a child and that she was very sensitive about it. We said we weren't sure which eye it was, but if he looked closely, he'd be able to spot it. Each woman was told the same story about her date. On their dates, the couples spent the evening gazing into each other's eyes searching in vain for the 'problem eye'. The outcome was that each couple reported high levels of intimacy and romance on their dates and the likelihood of the couple meeting again for a second date was 200% higher than the agency average.

When a woman likes a man, or vice versa, she will look at him a lot. This causes him to think that she likes him, so he will like her in return. In other words, when you are around someone you're attracted to, your gaze should meet theirs at least 60–70% of the time.

Her Body Language of Love

When talking to men, particularly in the early stages of courtship, women need to **reduce their facial expressions** so that they don't come across as overwhelming, desperate or intimidating. Most importantly, don't mirror what you think he *might* be feeling. That can be disastrous if you've got it wrong and you may be described as 'dizzy' or 'scatterbrained'.

His Body Language of Love

Men can make fewer than a third of the facial expressions a woman can make. Men usually hold expressionless faces because of their evolutionary need to withhold emotion to stave off possible attack from strangers and to appear to be in control of their emotions. This can make women think men are not listening or don't care. Women like to feel they are understood, so men should **mirror a woman's facial expressions** as she talks. Some men say, 'She'll think I'm effeminate!' but research with these techniques shows that when a man mirrors, she will describe him as caring, intelligent, interesting and attractive.

> Brain scans reveal that men can feel emotion as strongly as women, but avoid showing it publicly.

Check out what's under the table...

Want to know if a date is going well? Look under the table. Legs and feet are an important source of information about someone's attitude because most people are unaware of what they are doing with them and never consider faking gestures with them in the way that they could with their face. A person can look composed and in control while their foot is repetitively tapping or making short jabs in the air, revealing their frustration at not being able to escape.

Crossed positions reveal closed attitudes or uncertainty. A woman who is not interested in a man can fold her arms on her chest and cross her legs away from him, giving him the no-go body language, while an interested woman would open herself to him.

> Jiggling the feet is like the brain's attempt to run away from what is being experienced.

... but watch out for the Ankle Lock

The Ankle Lock. It's reasonable to say they won't be seeing each other again

When people are involved in a conversation, they also put their feet into the conversation. The **Ankle Lock** shows that someone is holding back a negative emotion, uncertainty or fear. The feet are usually withdrawn under the chair, showing that the person has a withdrawn attitude. It's the most common gesture patients use in a dental chair.

 **Tip:** If you're on a date and find that the other person has assumed the Ankle Lock, ask questions that will elicit a positive response. Our research found that asking questions was reasonably successful (42%) in getting others to relax and unlock their ankles.

Parties: how to avoid handshake horrors

Many men and women still experience degrees of fumbling and embarrassment in male-female greetings, which can get things off on the wrong foot. Most men report that they received some basic handshake training from their fathers when they were boys, but few women report the same training. As adults, this can create uncomfortable situations when a man reaches first to shake a woman's hand but she may not see it – she's initially more intent on looking at his face. Feeling awkward with his hand suspended in mid-air, the man pulls it back hoping she didn't notice, but as he does, she reaches for it and is also left with her hand dangling in a void. He reaches for her hand again and the result is a mishmash of tangled fingers that look and feel like two eager squid in a love embrace.

Tip: If you're at a party or social event and this happens to you, intentionally take the other person's right hand with your left, place it correctly into your right hand and say with a smile, 'Let's try that again!' This can give you an enormous credibility boost with the other person, because it shows you care enough about meeting them to get the handshake right.

Don't I know you from somewhere?

When meeting someone of the opposite sex for the first time, it's handy to use the **Power of Touch** if you want to be memorable. Touching a person with your left hand while shaking hands with your right hand can create a powerful result. Likewise, touching someone's hand when you pass them something makes people respond more favourably to you. Both actions will create a momentary bond between you. The touch must be discreet, though, or you risk coming across as creepy.

Tip: When you next meet someone of the opposite sex and shake hands, extend your left arm, give a light two-to-three-second touch on their elbow or hand as you shake, repeat their name to confirm you heard it correctly, and watch their reaction. Not only does it make that person feel important, it helps you remember their name through repetition. When passing a drink or coat to someone, allow your hand to brush theirs and they'll feel an instant positive connection with you.

Her Body Language of Love

At a party, everyone wants to check out the opposite sex and a woman's wider-ranging peripheral vision allows her to do this without getting constantly caught. For men, though, their **tunnel vision** means they will move their gaze up and down a woman's body in a very obvious way. This is the reason why men are constantly accused of ogling women's bodies but women are rarely accused of the same, even though research shows that women do more of it than men. It's not that men are bigger oglers than women – men's tunnel vision means they keep getting caught. Looking down towards the ground during conversation at a party serves different purposes for men and women. For a man, it lets him give a woman the onceover. For a woman, it has the dual purpose of letting her check him out and sending a submissive signal.

*Why do men have trouble making eye contact?
Breasts don't have eyes.*

His Body Language of Love

If you're a man and you want to find out which women like you at a party or social function, wear a neatly pressed suit and tie, but wear the tie slightly off to one side and put a little lint on one shoulder. Any women who find you attractive can't resist brushing the lint off and straightening your tie so that you look just right.

Wearing the tie just slightly off centre gives interested women the opportunity to straighten it

How to tell who's off the market at a party

If you're at a party and want a giveaway clue as to who is available and who is taken, watch their hips when they greet each other. The distance that two people keep their hips apart when they embrace reveals clues about the relationship between them. People who feel physical intimacy with someone press their torsos against each other and move within each other's **Close Intimate Zone**. This differs from the embrace received from a stranger on New Year's Eve, from your best friend's spouse or dear old Aunt Sally.

> The closer people feel emotionally to each other, the closer they will stand to each other.

We lean against other people to show a territorial claim to that person. Lovers hold hands or put their arms around each other in public to show competitors they have a claim over that person. A woman brushes imaginary pieces of dust from the shoulder of her husband to tell other women he's taken. It's not uncommon to see people doing this with people they are attracted to but not in a relationship with – it's a territorial message to others to stay away . . . or else.

'Hands off – he's taken'

Two's company ... three's a crowd

When three people begin a conversation at a party or dating event, they may begin in a triangular position but eventually two people may take the **Closed Position** to exclude the third person. This group formation is a clear signal to the third person that they should leave the group to avoid the embarrassment of being excluded. Other obvious signs that someone is being excluded include pointing your foot at another person you are interested in or crossing your knees towards them.

She's keeping her options open for now ...

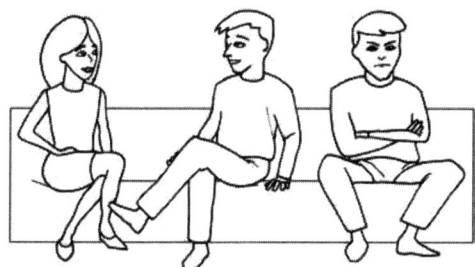

... but soon makes it obvious who she is more interested in

 **Tip:** In the above picture, the couple would like him to take a long walk off a short pier. The only way he could participate in the conversation would be to move a chair to a position in front of the couple and attempt to form a triangle, or take some other action to break their closed formation.

The man on the left is showing a complete courtship display, with his body erect and his thumbs highlighting his crotch. The woman is responding and showing that she is interested.
The other man should take a hike in the Himalayas

Body Language of Love
Rule No. 6

Historically, smoking has been used as another opportunity to emphasise our sexual differences: it allows a woman to display the vulnerable area around her wrist and open her body to a man and it allows the cigarette to be used like a small phallus being seductively sucked between her lips. The key to the perceived female sexual attraction behind smoking is the submissive attitude it implies; in other words, it carries the subtle message that a woman who smokes can be persuaded to do things that are not in her best interests. A man can highlight his masculinity by holding the cigarette secretively and seductively between finger and thumb. In many places today, however, smoking is as popular as a fart in a spacesuit, so as a general rule you should avoid smoking around the opposite sex unless they also smoke.

Body Language of Love
Rule No. 7

To be able to lie successfully, your body needs to be out of sight because your body language will eventually give you away. Consequently, lying is much easier in an email or online. This explains why so many otherwise honest people tell lies about their age, past and occupation on Internet dating sites and Facebook; lies that they wouldn't dream of telling face-to-face. Many people lie simply to increase their Mating Rating in the short term but can feel the need to come clean when they actually meet you because lying is so much harder face-to-face.

> On Internet dating sites, men exaggerate the criteria that are important to women: they lie about jobs, salaries, status and level of commitment to increase their Mating Rating.

Warning: The most dangerous liar a woman can encounter is the **Romantic Liar**. Some Romantic Liars specialise in concealing the fact that they're married, while others are expert at posing as lawyers and successful businessmen in order to extract sex or money from an unsuspecting woman. Romantic Liars thrive in Internet chat rooms and on dating sites. Our advice is not to automatically believe what others tell you. If you have any doubts, follow them up, even if this means asking an ex-girlfriend or hiring an investigator. Don't become a victim of romantic clichés or your own raging hormones.

For Better or for Worse: Finding a Long-Term Mate, Proposing and Dealing with Relationship Problems

'I want openness, honesty and a monogamous relationship. I'm not into men who want to play games'

Love starts with lust, which can last a few hours, a few days or a few weeks. Next comes infatuation, which lasts, on average, 3 to 12 months before attachment takes over. When the blinding cocktail of hormones subsides after a year or so, we see our partner in the cold light of day and those little habits we found so endearing at first can begin to become irritating.

> **When a man opens the door of his car for his wife, you can be sure of one thing: Either the car is new or the wife is.**

Finding the right partner means deciding what things you will have in common with someone in the long term, and to do this in advance of nature's blinding hormonal highs. When infatuation has passed – and pass it will – can you maintain a lasting relationship?

For many women, marriage is not for life any more. Life is too long. Marriage is for love.

How women can attract a long-term partner

Many women complain that men are only interested in casual sex and won't commit. By changing your body language and the signals you give out, you can be more confident of securing a mate who will be interested in you for the long term.

Play hard to get

In love studies, acting shy, bashful or coy was found to be very effective when used by women on men who were seeking a long-term partner. Coyness indicates that a woman could be hard to get and is seen as an indicator of fidelity which is high on men's criteria list for a long-term partner. If a woman is perceived as an 'easy lay', a man assumes that she'll also be easy for other men, which compromises his certainty of paternity. Playing hard to get is an excellent strategy as it appeals to a primitive male priority men want in women: fidelity and assurance that his kids are really his.

> 'Am I the first man ever to make love to you?' he asked. 'You could be,' she said. 'You look kind of familiar.'

For a man seeking a casual sex partner, coyness is a negative as it indicates that too much hard work or resources would be needed on his part. A woman who withholds sex raises her Mating Rating because it forces a man to look at her as a potential long-term partner.

> Marriages are made in heaven. But then again, so are thunder and lightning.

To look coy, a woman can try the **Sideways Looking-Up Smile**. With the head turned down and away while looking up with a half-smile, the smiler looks juvenile and playful. This coy smile has been shown to be men's favourite everywhere, because when a woman does it, it engenders paternal feelings, making men want to protect and care for females. This is one of the smiles Princess Diana used to captivate the hearts of people everywhere.

Show less skin

One study showed men and women a series of images of the opposite sex. The more skin a woman showed and the tighter-fitting and more revealing her clothing, the higher men rated her as a potential casual-sex partner but the lower they rated her as a long-term partner. The lower the cut of a woman's dress and the more she revealed of her boobs, the less the men could remember – or cared – about anything she said.

> The more skin a woman has covered –
> especially in erotic areas –
> the more likely she is to be perceived as a
> potential long-term partner.

How to tell if he's genuinely into you

The number one complaint of women everywhere is that they find it hard to tell whether a man is really interested in them or if he's just waiting for someone better to come along. This is partly because, in order to avoid awkwardness, many men will say they are going to ring a woman when they have no intention of doing so. So how can you tell? Watch out for these key body language signals and you'll never be left wondering if the phone is going to ring:

1. **Extended eye contact.** The longer we look at someone, the more interested we are in them. When the man's eyes dart from side to side, his brain is searching for escape routes, a sign he's planning his getaway.

2. **Touching and affectionate gestures.** Touching the hand or elbow, or hugging goodbye for longer than necessary are signs that he's serious about you.

3. **Body angling.** Is his body turned away from you, showing his desire to be elsewhere, or is he sitting directly facing you? A man will not only point his body or feet towards a woman he is genuinely interested in, he will also close the distance between himself and her.

Body Language of Love
Rule No. 8

Most people assume that hugs and kisses are always displays of affection, but gestures can be deceptive. If you are not too keen about hugging someone but are forced into it, you're likely to begin patting their back in the air even before the hug begins. The air kiss – with its accompanying 'Mwahhh' sound – is given as a displacement of a real kiss that we don't want to give. So next time you want to know whether someone's affection for you is genuine, watch out for those dead giveaways.

> People who are feigning affection will repeatedly tap your shoulder to break a clinch just like wrestlers do; sincere huggers hold on tight.

Perfect match?

Want to know if your beloved is your perfect match? Polish anthropologist Dr Boguslaw Pawlowski found that – in an ideal relationship – trust, money and respect are less important than the height difference ratio 1 to 1.09. His study found that, to ensure marital bliss, a man needs to be 1.09 times taller than his partner. This formula fits in the case of failed romances, for instance Nicole Kidman (5 feet 11 inches, 1.8m) and Tom Cruise (5 feet 7 inches, 1.7m).

Couples who fit this success ratio include:

Cherie Blair and **Tony Blair** = 1.10

Victoria Beckham and **David Beckham** = 1.09

Those who technically fail the test ratio include:

Camilla Parker-Bowles and **Prince Charles** = 1.01

Penny Lancaster and **Rod Stewart** = 0.97

Married life is very frustrating. In the first year of marriage, the man speaks and the woman listens. In the second year, the woman speaks and the man listens. In the third year, they both speak and the neighbours listen.

Body Language of Love
Rule No. 9

A study at the University of California showed that the most persuasive words in spoken language are *discovery, guarantee, love, proven, results, easy, health, new* and *you*. Practise using these words. The new results you'll get from the discovery of these proven new words will guarantee you more love, improve your health and give you great results with the opposite sex.

Marriage proposals... how to get her to say yes

A hundred thousand years ago ancestral man would return with his kill at the end of a hunting day and he and his group would share it inside a communal cave. A fire was lit at the entrance to the cave to ward off predators and to provide warmth. Each caveman sat with his back against the wall of the cave to avoid the possibility of being attacked from behind while he was engrossed in eating his meal.

Modern man reacts and behaves in much the same way at dinner functions as he did over a hundred thousand years ago. Businessmen and body language experts have long known that the seating arrangements, lighting and setting can have a profound effect on the outcome of any meeting. The same principles can be applied to marriage proposals.

Getting your girlfriend to accept your hand in marriage is far easier when she is relaxed and her defensive barriers have been lowered. This is why so many men propose on holiday, in expensive restaurants or in other romantic settings. If you are proposing at home, in a hotel or restaurant, here is the lowdown on getting that ring on her finger:

1. **Choose a venue with a fire:** Many top restaurants have an open fireplace or fire facsimile near the entrance of the restaurant to recreate the effects of the fire that burned at the ancient cave feasts.

2. **Have her sit with her back to a solid wall or screen:** Research shows that respiration, heart rate, brainwave frequencies and blood pressure rapidly increase when a person sits with their back to an open space, particularly where others are moving about.

3. **The lights should be dimmed and muffled background music should be played** to relax the senses.

4. **Obscure your beloved's view of other people** by a screen or large green plant if you want a captive audience.

5. **Remember the Power of Touch:** A light touch creates a momentary bond between two people. This is why a man will often take a woman's hand in his when asking for her hand in marriage.

Top restaurants use these relaxation techniques to extract large amounts of money from their customers' wallets for ordinary food, and men have been using them for thousands of years to create a romantic atmosphere for their women. It's far easier to get the answer you are hoping for under these circumstances than it will ever be in settings that have bright lighting, seating in open areas and intrusive background noise.

Trust . . . how to spot if your partner is lying to you

Trust is the foundation of any lasting, happy relationship, but how can you be sure you can believe what your partner is telling you?

The man in your life swears he's over his ex, but you know he has a picture of her in his office desk drawer. Your wife told you that she was out last night visiting her sick mother, but your instincts tell you something is not quite right. Are you being lied to?

> When men lie, their body language can be obvious.
> Women prefer to look busy as they lie.

One of the most valuable clues to discovering whether someone is being open and honest – or not – is to watch for palm displays. When people want to be open, they will often hold one or both palms out and say something like 'I didn't do it!', 'I'm sorry if I upset you' or 'I'm telling you the truth.' A man who wants to conceal his whereabouts after a night out with the boys might hide his palms in his pockets, or in an arms-crossed position, when he tries to explain to his partner where he was. A woman who is trying to hide something will avoid the subject while doing various other activities at the same time.

The main lying gestures to look out for are:

1. **Extended Blinking:** People under pressure, such as when they are lying, will dramatically increase their blinking rate in an unconscious attempt to block you from their sight.

2. **The Mouth Cover:** The hand covers the mouth as the brain subconsciously tries to suppress the deceitful words that are being said.

3. **The Eye Rub:** Lying men usually rub their eyes vigorously, and if the lie is a real whopper, they will often look away. Women will use small, gentle touching motions just below the eye.

4. **The Ear Grab:** This is a symbolic attempt to 'hear no evil' as the liar tries to block out the words being said by tugging their earlobe or putting one hand over their ear.

5. **The Collar Pull:** Lies cause a tingling sensation in the delicate neck tissues and a rub or scratch is required to satisfy it.

In isolation, none of these hand-to-face gestures necessarily means that your partner is lying to you, but if used in clusters of at least three, and if you get a hunch that the words and actions don't compute, it's more than likely that your instincts are right.

> To spot a liar, look for whether the person's body language contradicts their words. It's how you looked when you said it, not what you actually said.
> No woman believes a man who says, 'I love you,' while shaking his head.

Why women easily spot a lying or cheating man

Research by psychologists at Harvard University showed how women are far more alert to body language than men and that women are able to read a situation accurately 87% of the time, while the men scored only 42% accuracy. Women have an innate ability to pick up and decipher non-verbal signals, as well as having an accurate eye for small details. For survival reasons, women's brains are hardwired to read the body language of approaching strangers and of babies who can't talk.

> Being 'perceptive' largely means being able to spot the contradictions between someone's words and their body language.

Because of women's super-awareness of body language and voice signals, men get caught far more often, which makes it seem like men lie more. They don't. They just keep getting caught more. A woman's superior sensory equipment means that most men have difficulty lying to a woman face-to-face. But, as most women know, lying to a man face-to-face is comparatively easy, as he doesn't have much of the necessary brainwiring required to spot incongruences between her verbal and non-verbal signals. This is why few husbands can lie to their wives and get away with it and why, conversely, most women can pull the wool over a man's eyes without his realising it.

A man taking the ultimate lie-detector test

Tip: Most men, if they're going to lie to a woman, would be far better off doing it over the phone, in an email or with all the lights off and a blanket over their heads. Not only do women have a superior ability to uncover lies, they have the ability to remember them as ammunition for future arguments.

The rates of extra-marital affairs in most places are estimated to be 30–60%. The new era of text messaging, Facebook, online dating and 'affair websites' for married people have made it easier for both sexes to have extra-marital relationships. It's also made it far easier to get caught. Because women are better at spotting the signs of philandering, it's no surprise that even though over 80% of affairs are started by men, over 80% of relationships are ended by women.

What's the difference between lying to the taxman and lying to your wife? If you get caught, the taxman still wants to screw you.

Body Language of Love
Rule No. 10

Because of the stress associated with lying, a liar's voice can become more high-pitched. If your partner gets a text message on his phone from Charlotte and as he's explaining it's a wrong number or he's never heard of her, you notice he's chirping like a canary, add a tick to your suspicions chart.

Body Language of Love
Rule No. 11

Special imaging cameras that show blood flow in the body reveal that when a person is lying, their nose grows. Increased blood pressure inflates the soft tissue inside the nose and causes the nerve endings in the nose to tingle, resulting in a brisk rubbing action to the nose with the hand to satisfy the 'itch'. You can't see the nose swelling with the naked eye but it's interesting to note that a man's penis also swells during a lie. So if you're not sure whether a man is lying or not, pull his trousers down.

The Secrets of Successful Relationships

Women need affection

'Before we were married, he would hold my hand in public and rub my back. Now he never holds my hand and he only touches me when he wants sex.' Sound familiar? During courtship, a man touches his girlfriend more than at any other time in their relationship. This is because he is dying to 'get his hands on her', but he hasn't received the green light for any sexual touching, so he touches her everywhere else instead. When he gets the go-ahead for sexual touching, his brain sees no point in going back to the 'old days', so he just concentrates on the 'good bits'.

From birth girls are dramatically more sensitive to touch, and as an adult, a woman's skin is at least ten times more sensitive to touch and pressure than a man's. Female skin is thinner than male skin and has an extra fat layer below it for more warmth in winter and to pro-

Tip: To win points with your partner, use lots of appropriate touching but avoid groping, and be sure to cuddle your partner frequently and hold her hand to make her feel loved.

vide greater endurance. This is why women attach so much importance to cuddling those they love. In fact, a study with psychiatric patients showed that, under pressure, men avoid touch and retreat into their own world. More than half the women in the same test, on the other hand, initiated approaches to men, not for sex, but for the intimacy of touch.

Hold on to your woman

Today, there is a 50% chance a marriage will end and about an 85% chance the woman will be the instigator. It is estimated there are three suicides every day in the UK alone of men who are facing crippling child-support payments because the support system works on the principle that the more you earn, the more you pay. These men feel it's impossible to get ahead and get their lives back. So what do women want? Man's historical role as provider and hunter-gatherer means that a woman wants a man to show his long-term hunting potential and to share his resources with her.

> Marriage and love are purely a matter of chemistry. That is why one often treats the other like toxic waste.

Tip: Little displays of commitment mean a lot more to a woman than big, expensive gifts. Any action that demonstrates love is seen as a sign of commitment, so men need to show constant loving behaviour if they want to keep a woman. This means being caring and affectionate. Despite what Politically Correct activists may think, traditional gestures such as holding the door open for a woman, carrying bags for her and simply listening to her talking will go a surprisingly long way to showing you are in it for the long haul.

Smile, smile, smile

Smiling – or not – is a habit. Studies prove that you can dramatically improve your relationship when you regularly make the effort to smile and laugh to the point where it becomes a part of who you are. Relationships are more likely to fail when one partner not only does not mirror the other's expressions of happiness but instead shows expressions of contempt. The more you smile at your partner, the closer you will bond.

> **Research tip:** Only 15% of our laughter has to do with jokes. Laughter has more to do with bonding. Couples who laugh together, stay together.

Tip: To encourage laughter and happiness into your relationship, simple things like watching a funny movie or sitcom together, going to a comedy night or making a conscious effort to laugh at each other's jokes can pay real dividends. The more you laugh the more endorphins your brain will produce and the happier you will feel. And because of cause and effect, the more your partner will laugh too.

Men need to show they are listening...

Women often complain that men don't listen to them. Body language reveals a woman's emotional condition and accounts for over 80% of the impact in most female conversations. From a male viewpoint, women often seem to be waving their arms about and using a wide

> Body language is an outward reflection of a person's emotional condition.

range of facial expressions and gestures when they speak or talk on the telephone. Tone of voice conveys what she means and women communicate with a range of five tones – most men can only identify three. Spoken words account for less than 10% of the impact of her message. Consequently, words are not critical to female conversations because most of their messages are non-verbal.

Typically, a woman can use an average of six listening expressions in a ten-second period to reflect and then feedback the speaker's emotions. Her face will mirror the emotions being expressed by the speaker. To someone watching, it can almost look as if the events being discussed are happening to both her and the speaker.

Here is a typical ten-second sequence of a woman showing she is listening:

Sadness   Surprise   Anger   Joy   Fear   Desire

Here is the same range of facial expressions used by a man in the same listening period:

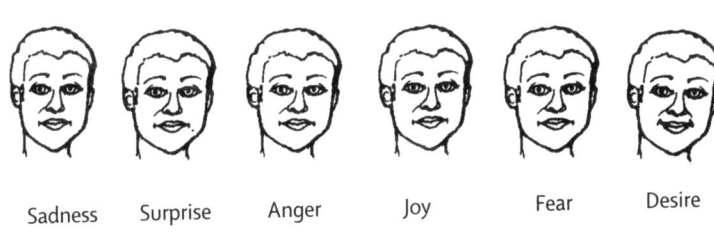

Sadness   Surprise   Anger   Joy   Fear   Desire

A woman reads the meaning of what is being said through intonation and the speaker's body language. This is exactly what a man needs to do to make his partner feel understood and heard. Most men are daunted by the prospect of using facial feedback while listening, but it pays big dividends for the man who becomes adept at it.

Tip: Rather than offering advice, try subtly mirroring your partner's facial expressions when she tells you about her day or something that is concerning her. And never define her words or interrupt her with the correct word. For women, emotions and feelings are what matter, and body language and tone are the main channels for this communication.

*'Once, I didn't talk to my wife for six months,'
said the husband. 'I didn't want to interrupt.'*

...and we mean *really* show they are listening

The building of relationships through talk is a priority in the brain-wiring of women. Contrast a woman's daily 'chatter' to that of a man. He utters just 2,000–4,000 words and 1,000–2,000 vocal sounds, and makes a maximum of 2,000–3,000 body language signals. His daily average adds up to around 7,000 communication 'words' – just over a third the output capability of most women.

This is why if a woman is stressed, she talks, talks and talks. She receives comfort and relief from the process of talking. The most valuable lesson a man can learn is to listen simply by using listening sounds and gestures. To a man, this is an alien concept because he only talks when he has something to say or a solution to offer.

An mp3 player has just been invented that can be implanted into a woman's breasts. This is because women complain that men spend too much time staring at their breasts and not listening to them.

The key body language gestures to show you are listening are the **Head Tilt** and the **Head Nod**. These are submissive and non-threatening, making others feel heard.

When a woman has finished speaking and feels you have heard what she has to say, she feels relieved and happy. Plus she'll think you're a wonderful man for listening, so you'll probably have a good night.

Men aren't great conversationalists, but they can at least learn to listen

Body Language of Love
Rule No. 12

When two people live together for a long time and have a good working relationship, they often begin to look alike. This is for two reasons: we are attracted to partners who look like us and successful couples are constantly mirroring each other's facial expressions which, over time, builds muscle definition in the same areas of the face. Even couples who don't look facially alike can appear similar in a photograph because they use the same smile. Successful marriages are ones in which both partners mirror the other's expressions and so learn how to be in sync.

Women need to pay attention to their appearance

He married her for her looks, but not the ones she's been giving him lately.

Like it or not, the way we physically look affects our ability to attract and keep a partner. In a long-term partner, a man is more interested in a woman's overall personality, intelligence and sense of humour than her body, but 'good looks' is still high on his list. Because visual cues are so important to a man, he unconsciously uses what a woman does or doesn't do with her appearance as a measure of her respect and feelings for him. He silently thinks if she spends time on her appearance, it means she wants him to be attracted to her.

One of the biggest complaints made by men in divorce proceedings is that after they were married their wives let their appearance go down the drain. They feel that she used her appearance to attract them and then felt this was no longer necessary after marriage. A woman finds it difficult to comprehend how a man can think this way because she will love him no matter how he looks. But that's the way it is for men, whether you like it or not.

 **Tip:** Many women become infuriated that their appearance can attract or repel their partner long after they've committed to each other, but it's a fact of life. It's also a fact that sometimes there is bad weather with thunder and rain, yet there's absolutely no point getting upset about it or complaining that it's unjust or holding a protest rally. Instead, you can prepare for adverse weather by having an umbrella, gloves or sun lotion. And so it is with the way men think. Don't fight men; manage them.

'Will you still love me when I'm old and grey?'
she asked. 'Not only will I love you,' he said,
'I'll email you, wherever you may be.'

AFTER MARRIAGE

BEFORE MARRIAGE

Above all, remember that men miss the details

Gail and Sean are driving home from a party. Nine minutes of silence have passed and he suspects something is up. 'Darling . . . is everything OK?' asks Sean.

'Yes. Everything's fine!' Gail answers. Her emphasis on the word 'fine' confirms that things are actually far from fine.

He thinks back to the party. 'Did I do something wrong tonight?'

'I don't want to talk about it!' she snaps. This means she's angry and does want to talk about it.

Meanwhile, he's at a complete loss to understand what he's done wrong. 'I don't know what I did!' he pleads. He's telling the truth – he simply doesn't understand the problem.

'OK then,' she says, 'I'll tell you, even though you're playing that stupid act!' But it's not an act. He genuinely doesn't have a handle on the problem. 'That bimbo was hanging around you all night giving you come-on signals and you encouraged her!'

Huh? Now Sean is completely dumbstruck. What bimbo? What come-on signals? An argument then ensues.

You see, while the 'bimbo' (this is a woman's expression; men would likely describe her as 'sexy') had been talking to him, he hadn't noticed that she was tilting her pelvis, pointing her foot his way, flicking her hair, stroking her thigh, massaging her earlobes, stroking the stem of her wine glass and talking like a schoolgirl. Hey – he's a hunter. He can spot a zebra on the horizon and tell you how fast it's moving. But he doesn't have a woman's ability to pick up the visual, vocal and body language signals that say someone's on the make. Every woman at the party saw what the 'bimbo' was doing – without even moving their heads. And a telepathic 'bitch alert' was sent and received around the room. Most of the men missed it completely. So when a man claims he is telling the truth about these accusations, he probably is. Male brains are not equipped to hear or see the fine intricacies of body language. Women have up to 16 locations in the brain used to evaluate others' behaviour versus a man's 4 to 6 areas. This explains how a woman can attend a dinner party and rapidly work out the state of the relationships of other couples at the party – who's had an argument, who likes who and so on.

Tip: If you're a woman and want to avoid arguments with your partner, remember that most men simply miss the details.

Men miss the details

Learn that honesty isn't always the best policy

When a woman asks, 'Does this dress make me look fat?' what is your answer? If you are a man who has had any experience with women, you'd say she looked good. But you might have been thinking, 'The dress doesn't make you look fat – it's all the cake and ice cream you eat that makes you look fat.' If you said this, though, she'd probably throw the best china at you.

In fact, if you told the complete truth to your partner all the time, you'd undoubtedly end up very lonely or in the divorce courts. Telling white lies is a vital part of maintaining a relationship. The goal of white lies is to make others feel comfortable instead of telling them the cold, hard truth. Always telling someone the complete truth will make you sad and lonely. White lies are the oils that grease our interactions with others.

The number one question men ask that makes women lie: 'How was I?'

 **Tip:** Learn how to tell white lies convincingly to your loved one by practising open palm gestures and head nodding. This will give the other person the feeling that you are telling the truth and being sincere, and will help you avoid a broken leg.

'Honestly, honey, sex with my ex was lousy'

Only enemies speak the truth. Friends and lovers lie endlessly, caught in the web of duty.
STEPHEN KING

The number one gesture all happily married men avoid

The thumb can be used as a signal of ridicule or disrespect when it is used to point at another person. For example, the man who leans across to his friend, points towards his partner with his thumb and says, 'She always nags,' is inviting an argument with her. In this case, the shaking thumb is used as a pointer to ridicule her. Consequently, thumb-pointing is extremely irritating to most women, particularly when a man does it. If you're a man and value your relationship, you should avoid using the thumb in this way. Women perceive it as a put-down.

'That's the old ball and chain over there'

> **What should you do if your old boiler breaks down?**
> **Buy her a bunch of flowers.**

Finally, work *with* each other's differences, don't fight about them

Our evolutionary roles have equipped us with the biological skills and senses we need for survival. Having evolved to be carers and nurturers, women are simply better at picking up the small nuances in body language, vocal cues, tone of voice and other sensory stimuli.

It's not so much that women have super senses – it's more that men's senses have been dulled, comparatively speaking. In a woman's world of higher perceptiveness, she expects a man to read her verbal, vocal and body language signals and to anticipate her needs, just as another woman would do. A woman quietly assumes that a man will know what she wants or needs, and when he doesn't pick up on her cues, she accuses him of being 'Insensitive – wouldn't have a clue!' No wonder 50% of marriages fail. The good news is that most men can be trained to improve their awareness of non-verbal and vocal messages. Women need to accept that they will not change the men in their life. For a happy relationship, we need to embrace and work with our differences, not against them.

> Men and women are different.
> Not better or worse, but different.

Conclusion

Communication through body language has been going on for millions of years, and is the keystone of our interactions with the opposite sex, yet when it comes to our love lives, many of us have lost the art. In all Western and European countries marriage rates are the lowest they've been in 100 years – half the rate of 25 years ago. In places such as Australia 28% of adults have never married. In the USA, 63% of all new marriages end. Online dating, IT matchmaking, flirt-a-thons and speed-dating events are booming everywhere. And because men have more difficulty than women in meeting the opposite sex, most flirting classes worldwide have more male attendees than women. Most of those who do marry or permanently co-habit struggle to make a relationship work in the long term, citing breakdown of communication, incompatibility, infidelity and 'irreconcilable differences' as the main factors. Men and women have forgotten the body language gestures and signals our ancient ancestors took for granted.

It *is* possible, however, to learn to communicate better through body language. Research has now shown that when you change your body language, it impacts on many of your attitudes in your approach to life. You can alter your mood before going to a party, feel more confident around the opposite sex, be more approachable and more attractive. When you change your body language for the better, you will interact differently with others and they, in turn, will respond differently to you. This is why understanding body language is so critical to your love life. Positive body language will make you feel better and look more attractive; it will benefit your relationships and reinforce the bond with your partners.

Two secrets to keep your marriage brimming
1. Whenever you're wrong, admit it,
2. Whenever you're right, shut up.

Body language can tell you whether someone is available or taken, interested in a one-night stand or a long-term relationship, attracted to you or giving you the cold shoulder; it can help you to build healthy, happy relationships, tell you if someone is cheating on you and help avoid arguments and conflict with your partner. We hope that *Body Language of Love* has taught you how to read people correctly and to give out the right signals at the right time. We hope we have helped you to discover the remarkable and positive impact body language can have on your love life.

Finally, here's a brief summary of the keys points for a successful love life.

The secrets of attractive body language in courtship

Face: Have an animated face, look approachable and open, and make smiling a part of your regular repertoire.

Territory: Stand as close as you feel comfortable. If the other person moves back, don't step forward again.

Use open gestures: Avoid crossed legs, ankles and arms, and keep your palms visible.

Eye contact: Use extended gazing on those you are attracted to, but be sure to give the amount of eye contact that makes others feel comfortable.

Highlight sexual differences to attract the opposite sex. This can be as simple as paying more attention to your appearance. Like it or not, how you look is important.

Women need to give clear, unambiguous signals to men they are attracted to, but avoid bombarding them with too many cues too early.

Men need to work to read women's body language more effectively: Women are adept at giving out courtships signals, but men miss most of them and therefore avoid approaching women with whom there is a mutual attraction.

The secrets of attractive body language in relationships

Men should give more facial feedback: Use Head Nods and Head Tilt when your partner is talking, rather than offering solutions.

Women should remember that men value attractiveness highly even after the courtship phase has passed.

Smile often, and make humour and laughter a key part of your relationship to build rapport and increase happiness.

Mirror the body language of your partner to strengthen the bond between you and create harmony.

Those who are 'lucky in love' understand that gestures and expressions are more important than what is said.

Research has found that the total impact of a message is less than 10% verbal (words only), 60–80% non-verbal and the rest is intonation. Unless you have an innate ability or have learned to read body language, the chances are that until now you've been missing most of what the opposite sex has been trying to tell you. Hopefully, this book will have shown you what you've been missing, and your love life will now go from strength to strength!

Why not use Allan Pease as guest speaker for your next conference or seminar?

PEASE INTERNATIONAL PTY LTD

PO Box 1260, Buderim 4556, Queensland, AUSTRALIA
Tel: +61 7 5445 5600

Email: info@peaseinternational.com
Website: www.peaseinternational.com

Allan and Barbara Pease are the most successful relationship authors in the business. They have written a total of 15 bestsellers - Including 9 number ones- and give seminars in up to 30 countries each year. Their books are available in over 100 countries, are translated into 51 languages and have sold over 25 million copies. They appear regularly in the media worldwide and their work has been the subject of 9 television series, a stage play and a number one box office movie which attracted a combined audience of over 100 million.

Their company, Pease International Ltd, produces videos, training courses and seminars for business and governments worldwide. Their monthly relationship column was read by over 20 million people in 25 countries. They have 6 children and 5 grandkids and are based in Australia and the UK.

Also by Allan Pease:

DVD Programs
Body Language Series
Silent Signals Series
How To Be A People Magnet - It's Easy Peasey
The Best Of Body Language
How To Develop Powerful Communication Skills - Managing the Differences Between Men & Women

Audio Programs
The Definitive Book Of Body Language
Why Men Don't Listen & Women Can't Read Maps
Why Men Don't Have A Clue & Women Always Need More Shoes
How To Make Appointments By Telephone
Questions Are The Answers
It's Not What You Say

Books
The Body Language of Love
Body Language in the Work Place
The Definitive Book Of Body Language
Why Men Don't Listen & Women Can't Read Maps
Why Men Lie & Women Cry
Why Men Want Sex & Women Need Love
You Can! People Skills For Life
Questions Are The Answers
Why He's So Last Minute & She's Got It All Wrapped Up
Why Men Can Only Do One Thing At A Time & Women Never Stop Talking
How Compatible Are You? Your Relationship Quiz Book
Talk Language
Get It Write

www.PeaseInternational.com